Martin the Guitar
ON THE ROAD

by **HARRY MUSSELWHITE**
Illustrated by **BRIAN BARR**

From Harry:
"Martin the Guitar: On the Road" goes out to Laura, Dory, and Austin, and especially national
guitar treasure Dan Crary, who got the whole "Martin" train on the tracks early on. Special thanks go to
Ron Middlebrook, publisher extraordinaire and valued creative force behind the "Martin" series.

From Brian:
To my wife, Carrie, for all her love and support, and to my mom, who still
wants to put my drawings up on her refrigerator.

Words and Story ©2017 by Harry Musselwhite

Illustrations ©2017 by Brian Barr

Art Direction and Design by Monica Sheppard

Many thanks to Mr. Dick Boak of C.F. Martin & Company for his valuable assistance in
the development and production of this book.

Visit **www.martintheguitar.com** for access to FREE downloadable music
to accompany "Martin the Guitar – On the Road".

ISBN: 978-1-57424-340-6

Published by

Centerstream Publishing, LLC
P.O. Box 17878 –Anaheim Hills, CA 92817

www.centerstream-usa.com

Martin the Guitar looked out over the huge music festival crowd and took a deep breath. He had been practicing with his new owner, Robert, for weeks, and now it was time to step out on the main stage and make great music.

The crowd cheered as Robert and Martin took their place behind the microphone stand, and Robert immediately began strumming a fast tempo. The kids in the audience immediately began clapping to the rhythm. Martin closed his eyes and smiled as he heard Robert's rich baritone voice soar over the giant festival field.

By the end of Robert's set, Martin's nervousness was gone, and he didn't want to leave the stage. This was what Martin had been waiting for all his life.

As Robert left the stage, the other performers slapped him on the back and shouted encouraging words. The festival headliner, Charlie, was entering the stage, and his harmonicas all looked up at Martin.

"Oh boy, that was some picking!" shouted Freddie the Harp.

"Groovy tunes!" said Boris the Bass Harp.

"You rocked!" said Toots the G Harp.

"Cool!" squeaked Lucky the High Harp.

Charlie looked down at Martin and smiled. He looked up at Robert.

"Nice guitar, Robert. Let's jam later today!"

"You bet, Mr. Charlie," said Robert

"Call me Charlie." said Charlie.

Robert and Martin were simply thrilled.

The backstage area of the festival was busy with musicians, sound engineers, and assistants scurrying here and there while they prepared for the next performance.

Robert took Martin to the instrument room and placed him on a stand.

"Thanks for the great sound today, Martin," said Robert, "I am so glad I bought you from Mr. Beninato!"

Robert turned and left the instrument room.

Suddenly the room came alive as all the instruments began to chatter.

Freddie the Harp looked out from Charlie's harmonica case and waved to Martin. "That was some fine picking today, Mr. Martin. Fine picking!"

Martin beamed. It was his first big festival, and he wanted so badly to do a good job.

"Do you and your harmonica brothers play a lot of festivals?" asked Martin.

Boris the Bass Harp looked out.

"We've been all over the world, Martin," said Boris, "we've got more miles than a Greyhound Bus!"

"How do you like Robert?" asked a banjo from Nashville.

"He treats me so nicely, " replied Martin, "and he shines me after every gig. Robert always keeps fresh strings on so I can sound my best."

"Our owners treat us the same way," said Alfredo the Accordian, "they know we can't do our best job unless we are in tip top shape!"

All the instruments murmured in agreement.

The instruments quieted down as the door to the instrument room opened.

A large man with a scruffy beard peered into the room.

"He doesn't look like he belongs in here," whispered the Banjo.

"I don't like it, " said Freddie the Harp.

Quick as a wink, the man reached out and grabbed Charlie's harmonica case, and as he ran out of the room, he grabbed Martin with his other hand.

The other instruments were helpless as the harmonicas and Martin disappeared out of the instrument room.

Martin and his friends had been kidnapped!

Robert spotted Harmonica Charlie talking with some fellow musicians across the backstage area. He ran over.

"Charlie, you are not going to believe it, but our instruments have been stolen!"

"Are you sure? Did you check with the stage manager?" exclaimed a worried Charlie.

"I have! Nobody saw a thing!" answered Robert.

"Come on, " said Charlie, "we'll get to the bottom of this!"

Charlie, his guitar player Lars, and Robert searched the instrument room from top to bottom. The instruments were nowhere in sight.

A very concerned police officer arrived, and the musicians left the instrument room in order to file a report.

When the men left, the instruments burst into talk.

"We gotta save them," said the banjo.

Suddenly all became quiet as a musican entered the room and put two cases down. He quickly left.

The cases opened and a large guitar stretched and looked out.

A smaller case opened and a mandolin did the same.

"What seems to be the problem here? " asked a guitar with a big loud voice.

It was Big D the Guitar, and standing right beside him was his sidekick, Loar the Mandolin.

The instruments crowded around Big D and Loar and told the whole story. Big D sat back and thought.

"Hmmm," intoned Big D.

"Hmmmm," imitated Loar.

Big D cut Loar a look, and Loar looked down.

"Loar, my buddy, didn't you hear me say just a few minutes ago as we were coming into the backstage area, "That scruffy fellow is carrying a guitar that looks like our old friend Martin the Guitar."

Loar answered, "You did, Big D, I'll say you did!"

"They ran into a tool shed down by the parking lot."

"Gather round, instruments, " said Big D, " we've got some planning to do!"

The tool shed was hot and dark.

"I can't see a thing, and it's hot as a Sunday afternoon gig in Brazil!" said Freddie the Harp.

Lucky the High Harp sniffled a bit.

"I want to go back to Charlie. I don't like it here!"

"Don't worry," said Toots, " Charlie will find us."

"We've got to stick together and be brave." said Martin.

"Yeh," said Freddie.

Martin was frightened but he knew he had to be brave for the little harmonicas. He had to stand up for his little friends.

Suddenly the door opened. It was the man. He looked all around the hot shed and smiled.

"I'm gonna get a lot of money for you famous instruments, so don't go running away!" he said.

The man laughed and laughed as he closed the door.

Boris the Bass Harp looked at Martin.

"I don't like this a bit, Martin!"

"Stay cool,' said Martin, "I am sure help is on the way!"

Martin tried to smile, and he whispered to himself, "I sure HOPE help is on the way!".

The day drew longer, and the stolen instruments could hear the music in the distance from the festival. As the sun set and darkness approached, they all became very gloomy.

The shed was dark as the music outside faded away. Every now and then Martin could hear the little "peep" of one of his harmonica friends, but mostly they stayed quiet.

Suddenly the door began to shake.

Freddie looked out.

"What's going on, Martin?"

"Shush," said Martin, "stay quiet!"

"I want Charlie," said Toots.

"Me too," said Lucky.

The door rattled even more, and the instruments became frightened.

"Help!" cried Freddie.

Suddenly, the door burst open!

In walked none other than....Big D the Guitar. Behind him was Loar, A banjo, and Alfredo the Accordian.

"Didn't think I'd let my best buddy go off all by himself, eh?" said Big D.

"Are you nice?" trembled Lucky!

"The nicest guitar you ever met, I mean, unless you count young Martin here!"

Big D laughed with his big belly laugh.

"D, I am one happy guitar to see you!"

"What about me, Mr. big time?"

Martin slapped Loar on the back.

"Of course, Loar," said Martin, "you saved the day!"

"Look, this family reunion is nice, but we gotta get out of here, and pronto!" said Big D.

"We are right behind you!" said Freddie.

The crowd roared as Robert and Harmonica Charlie brought their set to an end with a rocking blues number.

Robert looked at Charlie and grinned from ear to ear.

"Glad to have our babies back, eh?" said Charlie.

"You know it!" answered Robert.

Martin looked over at Freddie and winked.

All the musicians gathered back stage to celebrate the mysterious return of the stolen instruments. Now there was an official guard at the door to the instrument room. Charlie and Robert put up their instruments.

As they were finishing, a beautiful folk singer from California put her case on the shelf of the instrument room. The three musicians greeted each other and left the room to join the celebration.

Martin looked at Freddie and they both looked at the new case.

"Now who do you suppose this is? " said Freddie.

"You got me," answered Martin.

Slowly the black guitar case opened and a beautiful guitar sat up. She had long eyelashes and a beautiful shiny finish.

"Hello boys, " she said, "My name is Morgan the Guitar."